TRAVELLING
ART

Not a square inch left undecorated on this Open Lot waggon.

TRAVELLING ART

Gypsy Caravans and Canal Barges

JOHN BAXTER AND
GORDON THORBURN

The
History
Press

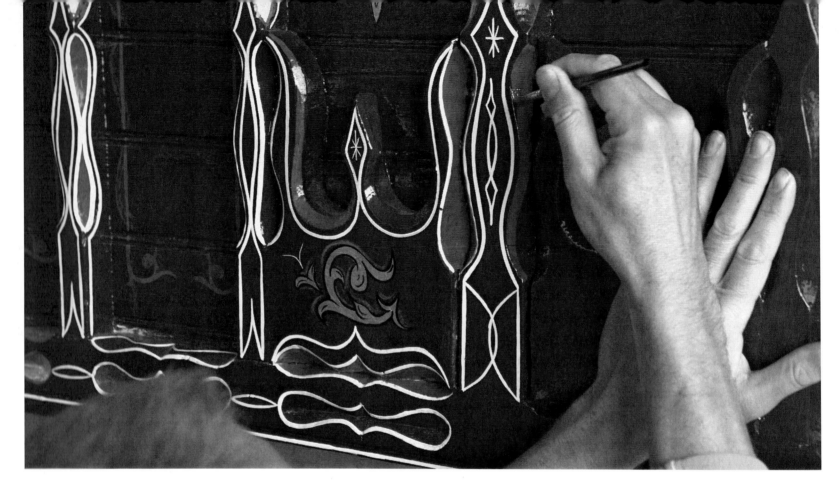

First published 2010
Reprinted 2014

The History Press
The Mill, Brimscombe Port
Stroud, Gloucestershire, GL5 2QG
www.thehistorypress.co.uk

British Library Cataloguing in Publication Data.
A catalogue record for this book is available from the British Library.

ISBN 978 0 7524 5502 0

Typesetting and origination by The History Press
Printed in Great Britain

CONTENTS

ACKNOWLEDGEMENTS

Many thanks are due to Rory Coxhill, Phil Varey and Maggie Roberts. The line drawings are by Sue Thorburn.

INTRODUCTION

The main purpose of this book is to explain and describe a phenomenon, and, while we can, to help preserve it by generating more interest. The phenomenon is 'The decorative arts as applied to small movable dwellings'. So small and cramped are those dwellings, in fact, that only those used to living in a tent would find an improvement.

If you were to live your life on the road, in a mobile version of a garden shed, what would you do to increase your happiness with it? Would you, for instance, spend a small fortune decorating it in gold leaf and Renaissance-style wood carvings?

Or, suppose you lived on water, in that tiny portion of a narrow barge not allocated to the barge's reason for existence – the carriage of goods. If the goods were mostly dirty or dusty, such as coal, quarry stone or grain, how much effort would you expend on showing the world the bright colours on the exterior of your home?

Travelling art on water had a very short time from development to near disappearance. On the road, the heyday of artistic life lasted much longer, all of seventy years or so. When the art's bases – the narrowboat as goods train, the gypsy caravan as cottage – ceased being practicable for modernity, the art upon them was kept in view only by tradition and sentiment. Thankfully, there was enough of that to enable us, in our world of instant image manipulation on screens of a thousand score of colours, still to look and marvel at what they did a century ago with a sharp knife, a brush and a pot of paint.

ONE

THE THOUSAND-YEAR JOURNEY

Who are these people, the gypsies? From the reader's point of view, looking and wondering at the glories of caravan art, the real question is probably not so much who the gypsies are, but who they were. No more do families buy horse-drawn art exhibitions instead of houses. There is no market for it. The life that demanded such style has faded away and cannot come again. Apart from a few dedicated restorers, the artist-craftsmen who earned their pay by building, carving and painting the caravans are just as dead and gone as Renoir. Their gypsy patrons no longer see the waggon as home. The mobile cottage is for collectors only, and for a few romantics who want to experience a piece of history. So, how did it all come about and where did it go?

———◆———

This is an extract from a novel called *The Gypsy Queen* in the British Girls' Library series, published at the beginning of the last century by S.W. Partridge & Co. at a shilling and sixpence (about £6 in 1900 purchasing power). The author, one Emma Leslie, obviously knew her readers well and how to pander to them. Her contempt, middle-class prejudice and schoolgirl venom seep from every sentence.

That text, written over a hundred years ago, describes one image of gypsies. Another, which D.H. Lawrence may have been exploiting in *The Virgin and the Gypsy*, added a certain romance and glamour to the

---

THE GYPSY QUEEN

The gypsy camp was in a clearing of the forest, and consisted of one or two dirty ragged tents, a few vans, and a heterogeneous collection of old lumber scattered round, with some half-starved looking dogs and bony horses and donkeys.

During the day an old woman and a few babies and young children were the only occupants of the camp, but as the shades of evening drew on, one and another, men, women and children, came in from various quarters, and active preparations for supper were commenced.

It depended very much on the 'luck', or opportunities for dealing, the inhabitants had had whether this supper was bountiful or otherwise.

Sometimes the man selling clothes' pegs would produce a fine duck or chicken, or the tinker would bring out a rabbit or a joint of meat; while the women who had been fortune-telling among the silly servant girls of the neighbourhood could generally produce half loaves of bread, portions of a cold joint or meat pie, to say nothing of artfully concealed bottles of spirits, without which no gypsy feast would be complete.

Then a couple of roaring fires were lighted, and big iron pots hung over them, and the various contributions of the fraternity were quickly turned into a savoury soup or stew, or if they had been out of 'luck', the snails the children had gathered during the day, eked out perhaps with a hedgehog rolled in clay and baked in the fire. Gypsies are by no means particular what they eat; if they were, they would very soon starve.

travelling people's otherness, their life outside society and their potential criminality; Robin Hood meets Clyde Barrow meets gentleman of the road.

The nearest thing today to a gypsy encampment is not one of those council caravan sites set well away from everyone's backyard, nor is it the New Agers in their 'clearing of the forest', but the gatherings at the big horse fairs such as those at Stow-on-the-Wold and Appleby-in-Westmorland, where some of the photographs in this book were taken.

There you will generally see one or two tents but not dirty or ragged ones; more likely they will be top-of-the-range frame tents with four bedrooms and a sun lounge. You might see a fire with a pot over it, but that is less likely than a six-ring propane gas range. Certainly there will be more than a few vans, but likewise with all the possible luxury extras and satellite TV.

These fairs are very popular tourist attractions too, although celebrity chefs hoping to glean recipes for snail stew and clay-baked hedgehog will be disappointed. There will be no half-starved dogs or bony horses either, and all suppers will be bountiful without the benefit of charitable half loaves or pieces of meat pie.

Given that prissy Miss Leslie's view of gypsies was somewhat jaundiced, it remains obvious that things have changed, but from what? We have few facts to go on, some legends and a certain amount of guesswork. The origins and early development of gypsies are not good subjects for scholars. There are no books, documents, charters or anything in writing to study, because the language and many dialects of gypsies were only ever spoken. There are no ruined buildings to reconstruct, no archaeological sites to dig up, no graveyards, no battles for throne or territory, no empires that came and went, no kings and queens, no burning, raping and pillaging, and there never were any learned gypsy priests to chronicle the news.

Without hard evidence, historians must turn to tales that are told – and tales that are told by gypsies about themselves have been related and re-related and passed on so many times that it would be miraculous if they bore any resemblance to the boring old truth. In any case, it would be most unusual for a gypsy, even if he knew such truths, to give them away to outsiders.

The most unlikely story believed by some gypsies is that they sprung from Cain, son of Adam and Eve and murderer of his brother Abel, sentenced by Jehovah to be a fugitive and a vagabond, yet with a mark on him that saved him from the full punishment due for his crime. One of Cain's descendants was Jabal, 'the father of such as dwell in tents, and of such as have cattle'. This is *Genesis IV xx*, and cattle as a term included horses. Another descendant was 'the father of all such as handle the harp and the organ', and another was 'an instructor of every artificer in brass and iron', all of which seems to encompass the musical, tinkering, nomadic, horse-dealing lifestyle of the gypsy pretty well.

Names are usually a good clue historically, but not in this case. The three main names for the travellers are *Tsigani* (Greek and central/eastern European languages), which makes *Zingari* in Italian, *Zigeuner* in German, *Ciganos* in Portuguese, and *I Zingari* in English wandering cricket teams. The more usual English word, Gypsy, occurs also as *Gitano* in Spanish and *Gitanes* on French cigarette packets. The third term, and nowadays the politically correct one, is *Roma*.

The first two are names given to travellers by the indigenous populations through which they came. *Tsigani/zingari* probably comes from the Greek 'athinganoi', the untouchables, but it is not clear if that is because of the Greeks' very low opinion of the travellers, or if it was by association with a ninth-century religious sect of Byzantium called by that name, *athinganoi*, which mixed Jewish and Christian beliefs and practices. 'Zingar' is also a Persian word for one who makes saddles and harness, which may be another way of explaining that name of the people – but not their origins.

Gypsy/*gitano* is a derogatory shortening of Egyptian. There are two possibilities usually given for that but they need not be separate. Egyptian was itself a derogatory term, used long ago for anyone thought to have magical powers. And/or, it could have come about because some of the early western European travellers said they had come from a country of their own called Little Egypt.

That the term 'gypsy' could have arisen from 'Egyptian' is easily demonstrated. The poet John Skelton used 'Mary Gipcy' for St Mary of Egypt in his poem *The Garland of Laurel*, composed in 1523, and he certainly was not referring to a traveller. Also, 'By Mary Gipcy' was an earlier oath, used as we might 'Gordon Bennett' or 'Bloody Nora'.

The travellers call themselves *Roma*, that is the European ones do, and there are two possibilities for this also. The first and least likely one is that the travellers, without an historical name of their own, adopted one from the people among whom they were living at the time. Whether they saw themselves as Romans or Romanians is not known. The other, more probable, option is that it is linguistic. *Rom* is 'man' in what is left of the travellers' language, called *Romanes*, sometimes Anglicised to Romany. *Rom* (*Romni* is woman) may be the same word as Armenian gypsy *Lom*, Palestinian gypsy *Dom*, and Sanskrit *Domba*, the name of a low caste of dancers and singers in Upper India.

Now, there is little doubt that the gypsy language is an old and fairly unmixed one, and that it comes from the same roots as all the modern languages now used in India and Sri Lanka. This may or may not prove that the Roms were originally the Doms, but it surely does tell that gypsies either came from India or spent a long time there. The *Oxford English Dictionary*, for instance, has them as originally Hindu, while other authorities are more circumspect. There is a theory that they were a Semitic or Levantine people, expelled by other, more powerful tribes – Assyrians, possibly – from their homelands in the Middle East, to wander through Persia and on into India.

Whichever version is true, it is probable that around the time the Vikings began migrating across the sea to new homelands in Britain and Ireland, other groups of people were leaving everything behind in India and starting a journey on foot, with no particular place to go, no route, and no knowledge of anything that might lie in front of them. That is, unless they were working on a race memory, maybe a thousand years old, and trying to get back home to the Levant, now that the danger had passed of the Assyrians coming down like a wolf on the fold.

For some among them, their unknown and unplanned destination was Britain, and the journey to first footfall would take them 600 years. On the way, many others turned aside and found their own places in the sun and rain, and they are still there – in Russia, Armenia, Moldavia, Poland, Finland, Sweden, you name it. Indeed, most of the families decided enough was enough at some point between India and Britain, but gradually – and largely by accident – a few of these families, greatly changed by centuries on the road, made it to the south coast of England.

Their forebears had been through Persia and Turkey, all over eastern and central Europe, into France and then across the Channel. Or, they might have gone the long way round, through Syria, Palestine, north

Africa and across to Spain. In any case, the first of the travelling people came to England in the fifteenth century, probably about 1435. This is an educated guess, based on an entry in the domestic accounts of the King of Scotland in 1505. If gypsies had reached Scotland by then, presumably they had taken some considerable time to work their way through England before that.

This is what the entry says: *April 22 item; to the Egyptians by the King's command seven pounds.* The King was James IV, a man who knew what was what, and if he paid seven pounds to some gypsies he must have been thoroughly convinced that they deserved it. According to average earnings of the time, that would be the equivalent of professional fees of £30,000 today.

Nobody knows what the Egyptians did to earn such an amount. Some think it was for entertaining the King and his court with music, dancing and fortune-telling. That may well have been part of it, probably along with a highly skilled pulling of the old pilgrimage trick, which went something like this:

Greetings, O mighty monarch of the glens. We are pilgrims from a strange land afar off, and we are on a long, er, pilgrimage, actually, through the whole world, all of it, at the command of the, er, Pope. Yes, that's the chap. The Pope. Anyway, give us your money and earn yourself a gold star on your heavenly report card.

It is amazing how well this trick used to work. A few months later, King James was writing to his uncle, the King of Denmark, telling him about that very noble fellow, Anthony Gagino, a Lord of Little Egypt and a pilgrim.

The next Scottish King, James V, seems to have been even more of a sucker for gypsies. He had them dance before him in 1530, paid them forty shillings (over £9,000 modern equivalent) and granted all sorts of privileges through a Privy Council writ to a certain John Faw, Lord and Earl of Little Egypt.

Elsewhere the writing was not so favourable. In fact, it was on the wall. In England in 1530, Henry VIII passed an Act of Repression:

...diverse and many outlandish People calling themselves Egyptians, using no craft nor merchandise, had come into this Realm and gone from Shire to Shire and Place to Place in great Company... that they by Palmistry could tell men's and women's Fortunes and so many times by subtlety had deceived the People of their Money and also had committed many and heinous Felonies and robberies to the great Hurt and Deceit of the People that they had come in among. From henceforth no such Person be suffered to come within this Realm.

The penalty for being found within this realm was taxation and banishment: confiscation of all property and fifteen days' notice to get out. The reason, as the King and his subjects saw it, was a good one. All nomads have to make a living off the land they pass through, and a certain shrewdness, a worldly wisdom, will always tend to accumulate in the brotherhood that wanders. The difference here was that Henry's Egyptians were not looking for good grazing at the next oasis across the desert. They had done so much wandering, and travelled so far, that a necessity had become a right given by the gods. Gypsies saw themselves as an elite, with the natural entitlement to live off non-gypsies.

If you are not a gypsy you are the Romany equivalent of a heathen, a gentile, a *sassenach*. You are a *gaujo*, *gadjo*, *gorgio*, and you are there to provide whatever it is the gypsy is short of just at this very moment. In our times, that generally means no more than it being perfectly all right to rip you off something rotten for your old copper water cylinder,

but, in days mostly gone by, it was all right to do more than rip off the *gadjo*. Gypsies, centuries before the French socialists, had their own version of that founding principle of so much left-wing thought: *Property is theft* (P.J. Prudhon, 1840). The gypsy version ran something like 'All movable property is thievable, until it becomes a gypsy's, whereupon it is for sale'.

No gypsy is supposed to steal from another gypsy and so, alas, they had to steal from the *gadje*, which was logical enough. Whatever the static, orthodox population might think was the accepted thing to do, and whatever laws they might pass to govern themselves and their property, and whatever the squire might believe about his rights of ownership over wild birds, animals and fish, the travelling man did not agree.

A gypsy today could not possibly accept that it was even the most microscopic misdemeanour, much less one of Henry VIII's heinous felonies, for a man to park his living-waggon on a piece of somebody else's grass, graze his horse on it, light a fire, and wade into the beck to lift a couple of trout. Gypsies of the sixteenth century took the same view, but apparently extended it to include silver spoons, purses, livestock and so on. Begging also was common but that was never a crime in India. You might also argue that the Christian Church was founded by a wandering beggar and is itself the biggest beggar of all time, but the worthies of Tudor England and Stuart Scotland found it a nuisance for all these gypsies to be going around begging, telling fortunes and helping themselves to fish and fowl.

By the last quarter of that century, that is from about 1575 onwards, the official view of gypsies as eccentric entertainers with magpie tendencies had given way to a much more virulent kind of intolerance. Just about every European country which by then had gypsies had also passed laws banishing them. There was nowhere left to be a gypsy.

In 1579, a new Scottish law proclaimed that:

Their ears be nailed to a tree, and cutted off, and them banished the country; and if thereafter they be found again, that they be hanged…the idle people calling themselves Egyptians.

In York in 1596, gypsy children were made to watch as their parents were executed (despite Henry VIII's Act, there were 10,000 gypsies in England in Elizabeth I's time).

In Edinburgh in 1611 they hanged four Faas (still a gypsy surname, sometimes as Faw) for 'abiding within the Kingdom they being Egyptians'. A few miles away at Haddington in 1636, the Egyptians got the same shrift:

… the men to be hanged and the women to be drowned, and such of the women as have children to be scourged through the burgh and burnt in the cheeks.

Gypsy Pearls

THIS IS ONE OF THE ORIGINAL ROMANY GYPSIES. SHE HAS TRAVELLED ALL PARTS. SHE HAS READ THE HANDS OF RICH AND POOR.

Genuine Romany

Please Step Inside

These laws, dreadfully harsh although not untypical of the time, were enforced only occasionally, and then because of some local incident. Gypsies carried on more or less regardless, and were frequently joined by non-gypsy outlaws and undesirables seeking comfort and friendship in a society of equals. It was a risky business though. As late as 1725 in Holland, some gypsies were tortured and had their heads cut off and put up on spikes to warn others away.

Things really did not improve until the abolition of slavery became general throughout Europe. Many gypsies had been made serfs, and even the ones who kept travelling and plying their trades were usually regarded, wherever they stopped, as the property of the local lord to do with as he pleased. In some countries, Russia and Spain for instance, gypsies did well and were tolerated and even appreciated. In others, like Germany and Romania, they were fiercely persecuted.

By 1850 or so, it was at least possible and permissible in almost all of Europe to be a free gypsy. Apart from occasional upsurges of anti-gypsy feeling there was only one more viciously serious attack and that was by Adolf Hitler, who sent many thousands to their deaths. In Britain there were many little local difficulties and almost universal prejudice and disdain, but the travelling way of life was feasible and it gradually acquired a kind of standard pattern and a romantic patina.

Gypsies could offer the rest of society certain useful and marketable products and services. First among these was everything to do with horses. News of the butchery in York may have travelled south, but a year later Shakespeare was writing *As You Like It*, in which Second Page recommends singing 'both in tune, like two gypsies on a horse', and it was ever thus. Buying, selling, breaking, training, doctoring, shoeing, harness mending and making, carts likewise, riding lessons, grooming and stable work – these were all second nature to the gypsies. One of this writer's acquaintance, called up to national service, found himself in a guards' regiment. The minute the commanding officer knew he was a gypsy, he was taken off ordinary duties and put in with the horses.

In an older world, driven by horses, the gypsy was a much-needed person, if not always properly valued and respected. Of course, there had to be a downside; gypsy skills at faking and disguising horses for sale were as highly developed and famous as their abilities to make a bad tempered horse good and a lazy horse lively.

Although some European gypsies became metal artists, highly skilled in gold and silver smithing, British gypsies did not. They were known for tinkering with pots and pans, a trade which seemed to lead naturally into scrap metal collecting as the tinker became redundant. Seasonal farm work such as haymaking, harvesting, picking potatoes, peas, fruit and hops were labouring jobs the whole family could do. Farmers also valued the gypsy's eye for stock and his doctoring skills with the old remedies. 'No job too small' could

have been a phrase invented by gypsies. If they were in the village, anything in need could be fixed, painted, sharpened, cleared away or replaced by the men, and the women could sell their families' output of clothes' pegs and lucky charms.

In other European countries, show business was perhaps more important than in Britain. Over there they had dancing bears, jugglers, acrobats, and they still have gypsy violins – whole orchestras of them in Hungary – and beautiful, dark-eyed girls swooping around the place with swirling skirts, castanets and flashes of bare brown limb. While their legacy is Django Reinhardt, Manitas da Plata and flamenco, we in Britain seemed to have ended up with little more than fairground rides.

Fortune-telling came with the very first gypsies from India, and it was logical enough to diversify into spells, curses and potions with attendant talismans, and to bring in whatever sales aids might improve the act, like crystal balls, tarot cards, palmistry, bump-feeling and so on. It should be noted that no gypsy ever tells the fortune of another gypsy, from the lines on the palm or anywhere else.

Here is a gypsy magic spell to defeat frigidity:

Take lemon balm, rosemary, lavender and sage, dry them, and grind in a mortar. On the night of the new moon, undress with your lover, throw the herb mixture on the fire, and make love on the hearthrug. As you lie together, both of you say:

Appleby Fair.

You herbs of love bring power anew,
May strains and stress be far and few.
Conjoin two hearts so love may flow
To end for e'er our nights of woe.

Do this every night until it is no longer
necessary.

Pardon me? Every night? So how do you tell when it
is no longer necessary? How many new moons are
there? Are you really expecting a couple, one lusty
and the other cool, to recite silly birthday-card words,
in unison, while romping on the Readicut? If one of
them is frigid, how do you persuade... oh, never mind.
They will probably do it on the wrong night anyway,

because hardly anyone knows that the moon is new when you can't see it at all.

Other gypsy ideas for promoting carnal activity include the lass serving the lad with cucumber and carrot for his tea, but not sliced crosswise. If that does not work – let's say he prefers sausage and mash – she should climb to the top of a hawthorn tree.... hang on, a *hawthorn* tree? Or, she could feed him the dried and powdered left testicle of a fox, while he feeds her the right one (honestly). If the lad ends up in a bit of a tizz – she loves me, she loves me not – he should place a stone on the left breast of her asleep, and when she wakes up she will tell him if she truly loves him. Well, use a smaller stone next time, you fool.

It is little wonder, then, in the age of science and cynicism, that a gypsy finds it difficult to make a bob or two in the traditional manner. Even into modern years, there were half a dozen Petulengros and Rose Lees on every seaside promenade, and charabanc loads of aforesaid servant girls and young farm yackers for them to feed on. Today you will be lucky to find one, but, if you do, please be careful. Cross her palm with plenty of silver, or she might write your name in black ink with a quill pen on a small piece of parchment, burn it, and blow the ashes to the four winds. And then where will you be?

All of these skills, crafts and ways of making cash have two things in common. They are transferable,

that is to say you can do them anywhere, and they require the amount and kind of tools and wherewithal that can be carried about in a caravan. They are the sorts of services that were useful and welcomed in small, rural communities, but only for part of the time. Few villages could have sustained a permanent practitioner. The gypsies turned up, they mended the village pans, knocked up a few stools and chairs, trained the two horses and the dog that needed it, sold someone a cart, bought whatever rags and scrap metal there might have been, picked whatever fruit or vegetable might have been in season, then moved on. Next year, they would turn up again at about the same time.

British gypsies, in that life they developed in kinder times, let us say very roughly 1800 to 1950, had their routines. Families and groups did not wander everywhere, but usually followed a circuit in a locality they knew well and said they lived in. Gypsies thought of themselves as from the New Forest, or north Yorkshire, or wherever. They might dive off for the Epsom Derby and Appleby New Fair, but otherwise they kept to the route that the family or small tribe had established as theirs. The villagers expected them to arrive and, when they did, business was done.

Now there is no need for such crafts and services. We do not mend pans any more, and we do not want a penny for a rag bag, and our potatoes are picked by machine. The horse job is dead, apart from horse riding for fun, and even the most conservative farmer will usually have more faith in the vet's antibiotics than the gypsy's herbs.

There are still a few productive occupations that suit the traditional marketing approach; hit and move on. If you go to Stow or Appleby, see what legends are written on the sides of vehicles: Lee Brothers, Roofing Contractors; Boswell & Son, Asphalting; Pinfold & Shaw, Painters and Decorators; Laws and Co., Loft and Cavity Wall Insulation; J. Crackles, Landscape Gardener. These are the twenty-first-century trades of the wanderer who has more or less settled down.

Instead of shoeing your horse, mending your jam pan, selling you a few clothes' pegs and liberating one of your chickens to line the iron pot, the new generation will tarmac your drive, and your neighbour's, then go down to the Moti Mohal for Chicken Tikka Masala in a microwavable plastic tray.

Those gypsies still travelling tend to be in scrap, or maybe knocking for bric-a-brac, garden furniture, bits and pieces. Times are hard in that game. Mugs who know not the value of their old possessions are getting fewer. Often the traditional gypsy expertise in horse-dealing and skills in metal-working have been combined to create a new career avenue in the fascinating and foggy world of second-hand motor cars.

So, what remains of the people who left India a thousand years ago? There are handsome, dark-haired women still, who like to wear bright colours with black and who state their place in society with the amount and splendour of their gold jewellery. Mega jeeps tow living waggons but they are huge, and done up to the maximum level of luxury, with more ornaments than a Victorian front parlour and more chrome than a dozen pink Cadillacs.

There are men with hats and waistcoats who are never without the necessary for a deal, whether that is a thick wad in the pocket or a solid gold ring weighing several ounces on the finger. They are also never without a nutmeg and a bootlace; a horse loves the smell of nutmeg, and will follow you anywhere with a bootlace tied around its tongue. The old values are still there: display your wealth; improve your possessions to the utmost; know a few things the others do not. But is there a proper way of life any more?

There are gypsies all over the world, in America, Australia and still in India where they started out. Funnily enough, there are very few in Ireland. The Irish tinkers, not from the same origins as gypsies but with a very similar philosophy, have rather more invaded the UK than British gypsies have gone over there.

Certainly in this country, whether you are a full Romany, part Romany, Irish tinker, New Age dole collector or conscientious refugee from the system, it is no longer possible to turn up anywhere and any time you like to camp for a week or two. Permanent gypsy sites have been tried; some succeeded and some failed. You can be quite sure that if such sites were in any way desirable to the *gadje*, they would soon be taken away, and so that in the long term does not look hopeful from the gypsy point of view.

No single strand of change in society can be identified as the one that caught the gypsies. We can blame the increase in regulation to the point where rules of themselves beget so many more rules that there is always a bucket full to throw at the gypsies. Big Acts, like the Town and Country Planning Acts of 1947 and 1962, and the Highways Act 1959, have little Acts upon their backs to bite 'em, such as the Caravan Sites Act 1960 and the Scrap Metal Dealers Act 1964. And little Acts have lesser Acts, and so do local authorities, most of whom are delighted to enforce every 'No Camping' regulation, but cannot quite see their way to providing the obligatory camping sites.

We can blame the massive increase in living standards and in standardisation of life among the ordinary static population. As a person's wealth increases, so does his intolerance of those unlike

himself in terms of values and ambitions. We can also look at the high-earning townspeople who have moved into rural Britain in pursuit of their urban dreams, and the country people who have increasingly left rural pursuits for salaried employment in the towns.

Whatever the causes, the habitats for most of the wildlife of this country have shrunk, and the gypsies are no exception. And it is not just the physical habitat. It has become more and more difficult to sustain even the idea of a freeborn people, outside the system, making a living by their wits and by turning a hand to whatever, moving around the country as they see fit. The rural Britain portrayed by the old black and white films, in which Felix Aylmer as the vicar perpetually clips his hedge while Margaret Rutherford freewheels down the village street on her bicycle with a basket on the front, was the sort of Britain that could include and cope with gypsies. It could tolerate them. Country people were never great enthusiasts for gypsies, but they did put up with them. Gypsies had their uses, live and let live, everybody deserves some respect and room to manoeuvre.

After all, there was not a lot of difference between ordinary, working village folk who drew water from a pump and gypsy folk who cooked over an open fire. In the early 1950s, when this writer lived as a small boy in Sheriff Hutton, near York, our source of water was a tap in the yard, or we could have gone to the pump in the street. We went further up the yard to the outside midden for other necessary purposes. Mother cooked on a coal-fired range. Although we had electric light, our standard of living was basically long stretches of monotonous 'just enough', occasionally interrupted by sudden surges of plenty when a piece of pork arrived in exchange for a favour, or father came back with a brace of pheasants and a rabbit.

Such a life was nothing to crow about. Nobody who lived like us could look very far down on the gypsies, and almost everyone in villages did live like us. They do not any more. The people who inhabit villages now are far more likely to complain about gypsy washing being hung on a hedge, horses being tethered in the lane and people doing in a field what we used to do on a wooden seat above a midden.

As the system has grown and absorbed the majority of the great British public and wired them into its information highways, so to be a member of an unchanging, non-conforming minority has become gradually impossible. While the gypsy minority has had to retreat, viewing its fate with horror, it has cried out and bitten back. As the suburbs covered the country and every open space in every village was filled by a new bungalow, the gypsies once again were back in the seventeenth century. They could find nowhere to be gypsies and they did not like it.

Even so, the fuss made by gypsies who did not want their entire life to disappear seems minimal. If there are no pumps now in the village, where does the nomad get water? From somebody's house? But if the office worker, washing the car on Sunday morning in the driveway, refuses to give the 'gyppo' some water, what is the 'gyppo' supposed to do? Tug his forelock? If the travelling scrap dealer cannot stay in the lane for a few days until his flat cart is full, then he must stay on a designated site with many other scrap collectors for months and months. Is there any wonder that the site becomes a scrap heap? And the scrap heap, of course, cannot be tolerated.

Gypsies of the 1950s and '60s who changed from horse to lorry, from *vardo* to metal-and-Formica trailer caravan, and from free firewood to expensive bottled gas, did so mostly in the belief that they were only changing the means. What they were really doing was signalling the end, which by now has been and gone, leaving us with 'a few vans' – museum pieces and private collectors' delights that once were commonplace. There are holiday homes, too, authentic caravans where you can have your organic breakfast brought to you in bed, with shower and toilet block nearby. Well, we should be pleased at anything that helps preserve a work of art.

TWO

ROMANI VARDO – FIVE WAGGONS TO PAINT

From the mid-fifteenth century when they first arrived in Britain, until the mid-nineteenth, by which time McAdam and Telford had revolutionised the roads, British gypsies lived in tents. A few still do, and the traditionally minded Romany was slow to convert from the bender to the caravan, but, by about 1880, most had embraced the compact luxury of the horse-drawn living waggon or *vardo*, a standardised mobile home designed from necessity.

There are species and varieties of *vardo* but only one genus, built around a single room with a stable-type halved front door. Although decor and quality of goods may vary, the internal layout is almost always the same whatever the style of waggon. It is an arrangement developed over the years and found to be the best compromise between comfort, necessity and lack of space. This single room has a built-in double berth at the far end with a kind of cupboard below for the children to sleep in. If the children were too many and/ or too big, they slept under the waggon or in a bender.

Another seat and some various cupboards, possibly including a display cabinet for the prize china and framed photographs, are on the right as you look through the door. A wardrobe, airing cupboard and seat with storage are on the left, as well as a stove. This was used mainly in the winter and bad weather, and, in the early days anyway, for heating rather than cooking. Except in impossible circumstances, cooking was done on a fire outside. Better designs of stove led to more cooking inside.

There are steps which pull up, more storage and racks on the outside and beneath, and the entire vehicle with contents, about 10ft long and 4ft 6in wide at floor level swelling to over 6ft at the roof, weighs a ton to a ton and a half. This was viewed as a reasonably comfortable draw for one horse, although we can be sure that nobody ever asked the horse what she understood by 'reasonably comfortable'.

Holidaymakers today, tempted by the ideal vision of a walking-pace, horse-drawn, sunlit wander around country lanes, might imagine that the horse will know her business and all the driver has to do is hold the reins and say 'whoa' occasionally. Such lack of horse knowledge explains why the firms supplying these kinds of holidays tend to be based in England's flatter counties.

The truth for a gypsy was somewhat different. The van was not a Post Office van or a grocer's van, delivering things, or a cabriolet carrying two persons and a driver. It was a home. It was a small country cottage on wheels. It contained all the necessities, and it was a home that had to go up and down whatever hills presented themselves. Going uphill, pulling a house, is very hard work and the horse might not be keen. If she stops, maybe the waggon will roll back. Going downhill, the waggon will want to run over the horse.

Almost anything can spook a horse. On the level, such an event could result in a violent start, sending household contents flying about, maybe even careering out of control, finishing with a crash through a hedge and a waggon on its side. Most waggons

were fitted with a variety of devices for braking and dragging, but, for those twenty or so miles a day, understanding of horse psychology was the most pressing issue and principal matter of all.

The moment a gypsy had a waggon, it became his most important and visible possession and a clear indicator of wealth and status, but, because one horse was the only practical number, he could not state his pride by size. It had to be done through style and decoration.

The high point in caravan building and painting was roughly from 1895 to 1925. The horse-drawn life looked to be pretty well finished by 1950, although some vans were still in regular use in the late 1960s.

This type of two-wheeler is called a pot cart, after those used by certain gypsy families who traded with the potteries of Stoke – see page 40.

Gypsy caravan building does not have a long history, but it has managed to acquire a great deal of folk-tale and fable, largely through the gypsies' inclination to truth-embellishment when talking to the *gadje*. In rural areas you will still find folk who believe that gypsies made each waggon out of 365 pieces, and that the roofs of the Bowtop type were made from the skins of otters snared by these cunning and swarthy poachers. There was no use trying to rob a gypsy caravan, because valuables were hidden in secret hidey-holes so cleverly concealed that no numbers of *gadje* could ever find them. Had they tried, they might have found the valuables but they would never have found the hidey-holes.

All this is pure fantasy because the gypsies did not make their waggons, apart from a few poor DIY 'peg-knife' jobs, and apart from the earliest vehicles, drawn by several horses, and used by showmen to transport themselves and their menageries of exotic animals. Showmen and Romanies did not recognise each other as of the same race, and, while the showmen might have built crude forerunners of the *vardo* around the start of the nineteenth century, the Romanies stayed in their benders.

Later, most gypsy families bought from particular coach builders who had seen the opportunity, specialised and developed their own *marques*. Names such as Dunton, Howcroft, Wheeler, Watts, Varney,

Tong and Wright may not have rung so loudly down the years as Rolls-Royce, Jaguar, Wolseley or Bentley, but their work was every bit as classy and distinctive; more so, since every *vardo* was custom built.

The great conundrum of waggon building was strength and durability balanced against weight. The need to get the waggon into – and out of – all sorts of difficult places, decided the size. The minimum living requirements of a family, such as a stove to cook and heat, beds to sleep in, seats, storage and so on, decided what the interior fittings would be, although there were differing degrees of luxury and high finish.

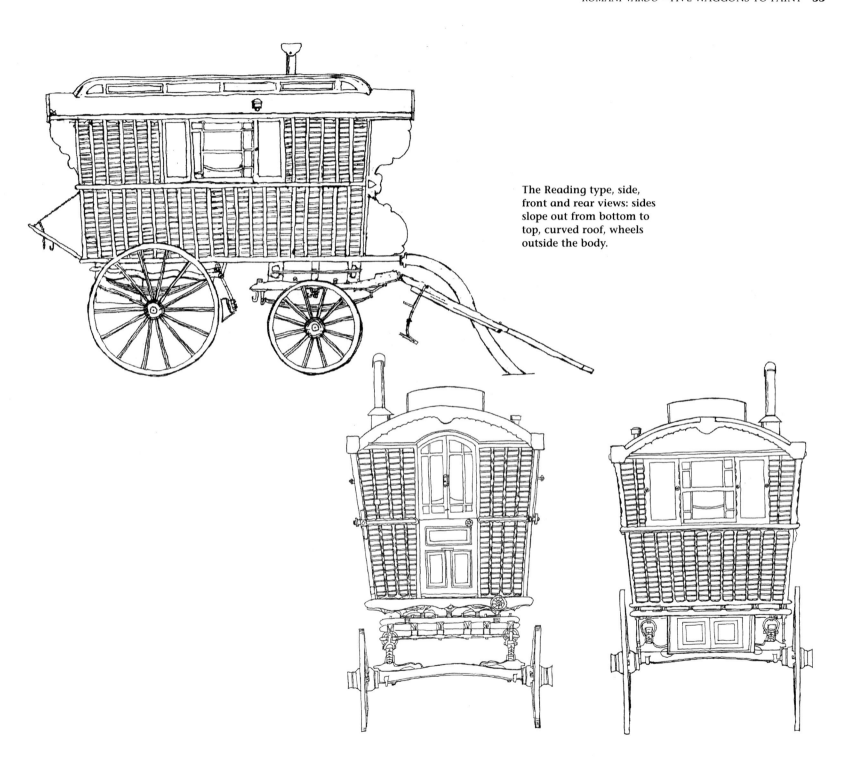

The Reading type, side, front and rear views: sides slope out from bottom to top, curved roof, wheels outside the body.

The Ledge type has a special elegance: narrow base
expanded higher up, wheels outside the base but
under extra body width, arched roof.

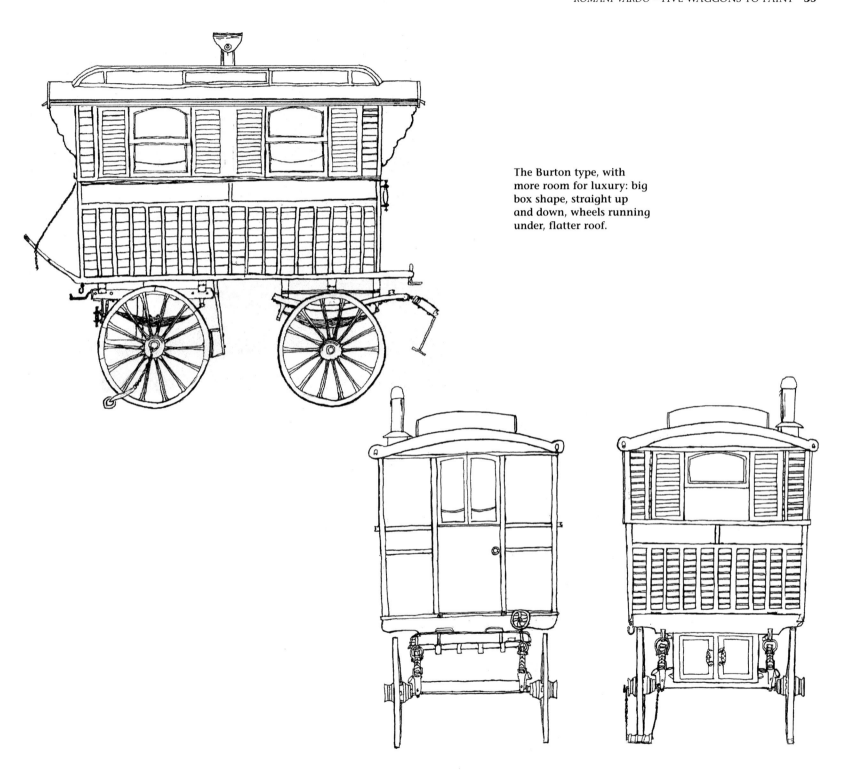

The Burton type, with
more room for luxury: big
box shape, straight up
and down, wheels running
under, flatter roof.

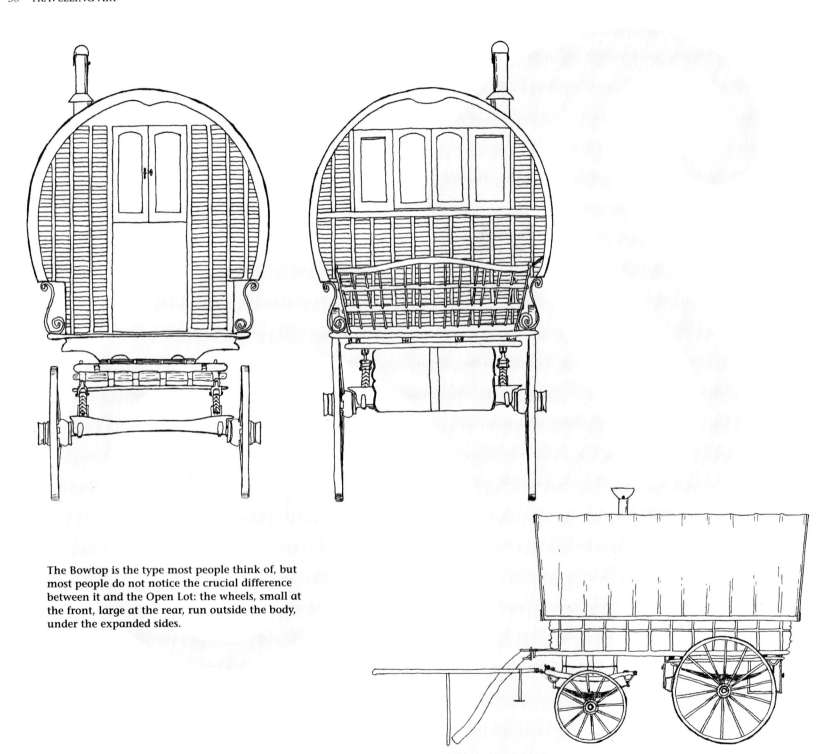

The Bowtop is the type most people think of, but most people do not notice the crucial difference between it and the Open Lot: the wheels, small at the front, large at the rear, run outside the body, under the expanded sides.

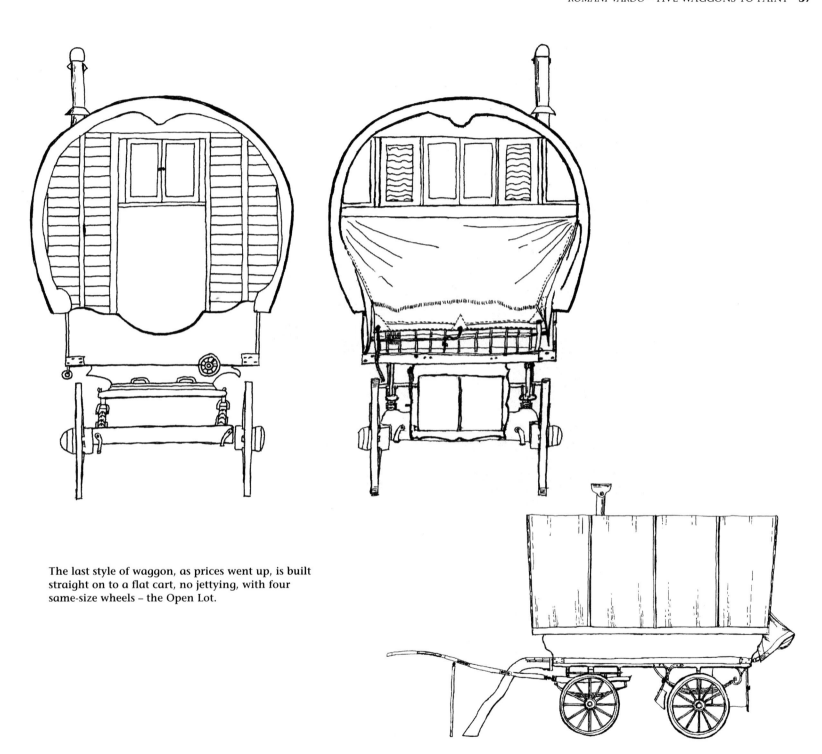

The last style of waggon, as prices went up, is built straight on to a flat cart, no jettying, with four same-size wheels – the Open Lot.

The one-horse limit decided the weight, so the only possible building material was wood, with minimal use of metal where absolutely necessary such as the springs, axles and the greased ring-plates that the front wheels, the fore-carriage, swivelled on for steering.

The basic frame, called the 'unders', was made of ash. The wheels had elm hubs, oak spokes and ash rims, with iron tyres, which was usual wheelwright practice in coach building. The wheels of firemen's escape ladders were made in exactly the same way. The horse's shafts were ash; the roof was waterproofed with several layers of painted linen. The main bodywork was tongue-and-grooved pine on vertical ribs, or sometimes rib and panel pine for the Ledge and the Burton types. Ash, sycamore, mahogany and oak were deployed for special needs – for example, ash for curved members, or sycamore for certain carved pieces.

Clearly, if your mobile home was going to last and withstand the rigours of the open road, the wood had to be of the best quality, cut and shaped with supreme precision and seasoned fully – double-seasoned, actually, since it always went through a second waiting time after being sawn. The purchaser, going to a reputable builder, would be confident of the high quality of components. No craftsman building anything as elaborate as a gypsy waggon would insult his own workmanship with inferior raw materials. Well, hardly ever.

There were five types of traditional one-horse living waggon plus one modern variant, all with similar internal layout but with many subtle and arcane outside details to differentiate the design and construction. The most highly regarded was named after its place of origin, the 'Reading', possibly not invented but certainly developed and built to fame by Dunton & Sons of Reading. Dunton's built other types too, notably the 'Ledge', and other firms also built the Reading, which had high, straight sides that slope outwards to an arched roof. The wheels – large at the back, small at the front – ran outside the body.

The Ledge waggon, also called the 'Cottage', had a much narrower floor but the sides were jettied out to a full width at about 18in up, and the wheels – again large at the back, small at the front – ran under this jetty, giving the whole vehicle a rather dainty appearance.

Both the Reading and the Ledge, with their slim bodies and high rear wheels, were meant to negotiate bridleways, fords, muddy back lanes, overhanging trees and the inconveniences of the countryside. The showmen families, travelling only from town to town, tended towards the 'Burton' type, originally from George Orton, Sons & Spooner of Burton-on-Trent, a bigger and bossier affair, a box with much bigger floor space at 6ft wide, slung high over medium-size wheels. One horse could pull it, but only on good roads. Later models got too big for that and had to be taken between fairgrounds by traction engine and petrol lorry.

Leisure vans began in 1885 with The Wanderer, 'the first purpose-built touring caravan', seen here being dragged out of soft ground by helpers while the gentry looks on. The designer of The Wanderer, Dr William Gordon Stables, admired the gypsy lifestyle and wanted to live it himself for a few weeks in the year, but seemingly forgot about the poor horse that had to pull his over-sized and over-fitted monstrosity.

The Caravan Club, formed in 1907, celebrated its centenary without a single mention of those travelling people its 370,000 family members are imitating. Now in the UK there are about 2 million people who go caravanning, camper-vanning and trailer-tenting for their holidays. To all of them and everyone else we say, read, mark, learn and inwardly digest. This is how it was.

The 'Brush' waggon, also called the 'Fen', was similar to the early Reading models in design, with wheels outside the body, but it had its door at the back rather than the front. It was much more of a travelling warehouse than home sweet home, and was not usually decorated very much because nobody would have seen through to it, so festooned and hung was the waggon with brushes, baskets, mats, all kinds of wickerwork, and things for making and repairing brushes, baskets, mats and wickerwork. Possibly because they belonged to the gypsy lower classes and as such were workaday vehicles with no artistic merit, it is widely believed that none have survived, although there is one (almost certainly the only one) in a private collection in East Anglia.

The 'Bowtop', made mainly in the north and midlands, had a jettied base and wheel arrangement like the Ledge waggon, but a top made of ash hoops with a double layer of carpet or felt and waterproofed canvas stretched over. It had less scope for external fancy but it was lighter, more stable on the move and much cheaper to build. It had no side windows, but that made it less noticeable at night.

As costs rose, especially wages for skilled tradesmen, another, final type was born in the 1930s from the need to keep prices down. The 'Open Lot' or 'Yorkshire Bow' was the prefab *vardo*. You got hold of a standard working cart or dray with four wheels the same size and built your coachwork and interior on that. The idea may have come from the much older 'pot cart', not properly a living waggon although sometimes used for sleeping. Before the canals and railways took all the business, certain gypsies used to buy cartloads of seconds from the Stoke potteries and sell them around the country. Their warehouses were these carts, flat-bedded with a retaining ledge around and a bowed canvas roof called a 'tilt'.

The modern variant of the Open Lot is the one you hire for your holidays, a living waggon built on a flat cart with motorcar wheels, brightly painted maybe but not really decorated like the old days. These caravans were built to last, and, as you can see from this book, some of them have. You can look at them at the horse fairs, the steam rallies and in museums. They are masterpieces of woodcraft and artistry and the very best of them, when new, cost as much as a small house. Unlike any small house, half of the cost – should the owner so choose – could have been in the art.

THREE

THE EYE OF THE BEHOLDER

While the reasons behind the art of the gypsy caravan lie in the lifestyle, tastes and attitudes of the people paying for it, British canal boat decoration had an entirely different regulator: business. We in this country have never had the possibility of a ship-canal system such as the mainland Europeans built, because we do not have the geography. We do not have the massively long and conveniently placed rivers to link together, so we cannot sail 1,000-ton vessels along our equivalents of the Rhine, the Danube and the Dortmund-Ems canal.

We did not get going at all on canals until three or four hundred years after the lock was invented (the timing depends on whom you believe invented it, the Dutch or the Italians), to allow canals at different heights to be linked together. We had a few relics left by the Romans, such as the Foss Dyke that runs for eleven miles in Lincolnshire between the Trent and the Witham, although the origins there are doubtful since the Norman king, Henry I, is also supposed to have had it built in 1121. Either way it is a tautology, since the Latin for ditch is *fossa* and the French is *fossé*. Take your pick, adding the interesting note that the Caer Dyke, now filled in, used to run from the Witham end of the Foss Dyke in Lincoln to Peterborough, and was supposedly constructed by legionaries on the orders of the Emperor Claudius.

In any case, no matter how ancient the history of our canals might be, there is no doubt about where the boom in canal building began, and that was in coal transport. The Duke of Bridgewater had collieries at Worsley, a few miles north-west of Salford, and he wanted to get his coal to Manchester. The work began in 1759 under the supervision of the engineer James Brindley. The canal opened in 1761, and the eyes of every coal owner and quarry master were opened immediately afterwards.

Canals had to be dug by hand (by navigators, or navvies); there are few areas of industrial Britain flat enough to do without locks, tunnels and aqueducts, and business demands speed. Consequently, the canals those navvies dug were narrow and shallow, suitable only for long, narrow, flat-bottomed barges, but not so long that they could not manage the corners. They were basically floating holds, with large hatches to simplify loading and unloading, and very little deck area.

As the canal network extended and journeys were not necessarily just from A to B and back again, bearing in mind the top horse-drawn speed was three miles an hour, the notion came about for bargemen to live on the job. It can easily be imagined that a coal-owner's idea of suitable quarters for a bargee family, on a small boat built at some expense to carry his lordship's coal, would not have extended beyond the very minimum.

Still, the canal business burgeoned – until the railways came and took it all away. This outcome did not happen quickly, of course, and a fight was put up, mostly involving cost-cutting which, eventually, made necessary some Parliamentary action.

The Canal Boats Act of 1877 dealt with all manner of things, including the health and education of boat-people's children, but its single most radical reform was to enforce the registration and inspection of every boat that had living accommodation and was working the canals. Since competition from the railways revolutionised freight transport, the canal industry had been largely characterised by low wages and poor upkeep of the boats, a combination that inevitably led to poverty and squalor. Now the boats had always to be in a condition fit for their purpose, including their purpose as residence, which in turn included standards of maintenance – regular painting, for instance.

At least, that was the idea. Many boatmen did not want their children to be attached to a particular school; they preferred their children to act as horse-leaders and lock-openers. The inspectors, health officials of the local authority, had no powers of arrest no matter how insanitary a boat they might find. The result, at first anyway, was a lot of boats disappearing into the sunset after inspection, and very little progress.

As the Act did begin to take hold, boat-dwellers found a pride in their horse-drawn homes, and a new system of decoration sprung up that rapidly became a tradition. The first step was a simple one, of painting the different parts of the boat in different colours – deck, sides, mouldings, hatches, green, red, blue, yellow, white, whatever took the fancy. Motifs were added in a fairly narrow range that soon became set as the accepted ones to have: playing cards, lots of diamonds and patchwork shapes made up of diamonds, compasses, castles, roses, moons, stars, ropes, and names painted on scrolls. Before long, decoration extended to the movables, like the water cans.

Why these particular designs became the standard is a bit of a mystery. We can see where ropes come in, and there is always a heraldic influence as with pub signs, but why roses and castles should be so popular we cannot know. We can say that the style was folk rather than fine art, and that the colours were unsubtly bright and cheerful. Like the gypsies in their vans, the barge people may not have known much about art but they knew what they liked. That, however, is the only link between the two communities, apart from similarities in lifestyle. They both lived in a very small space pulled by a horse, and had travelling as an essential to their earning money, but there was no mingling, artistically or otherwise. The birds and grapes never made their way onto the barges, and the roses and castles were not adopted by the van builders.

In Great Britain and Ireland there are about fifty canals and navigable rivers, with locks, tunnels and angles of bends in considerable variety. The boats they use on the River Barrow in Eire, for example, built to carry 50 tons of sugar beet, would be too large for the Kennet and Avon, while the crew of a standard English narrowboat would have a very exciting time coping with the huge drops and river-impelled flow of the Barrow locks.

Whatever the differences in boat design might be across these islands, there were always the same governing principles: to have as large a hold as possible, and to have as large a hatchway as possible above it, that is the absolute minimum of decking, for quick, easy and cheap loading and unloading. That these principles were incompatible with creature comforts for the bargees and their families was not a factor that unduly worried the barge owners. Space under decks – called 'cupboard space' – had to be cut to the bone.

The narrowboats that we recognise today began to appear around the start of the nineteenth century. They were built of oak, with iron ribs called 'knees', and their flat bottoms were elm until later, when steel became commonly used. The tendency of anything with a cup-shaped cross section is to collapse outwards, but permanent cross members on a narrowboat would interfere with business so there were movable ones – sometimes iron chains, sometimes rigid wood and iron – that could be unshipped when collecting or delivering.

Up at the bow end there was a small foredeck, giving cupboard space for stowing various bits of tackle including the ropes and tarpaulins for sheeting cargoes from the weather. They would also keep the food for the horse in there. At the stern was an even smaller deck, a little triangle on which the bargee stood to steer with his massive rudder, of a design called the ram's head, and in front of the tiller was a pair of doors, leading to the tiny palace below.

Nowadays, on narrowboats converted for pleasure, the first thing you see going below is the engine. In horse-drawn times, you saw a stove on your left, which discharged through a removable chimney. As with caravans in country lanes there were many obstacles on canals that could knock off a chimney.

Beyond the stove was the furniture, consisting chiefly of a food cupboard on the left that could double as a table with its drop-down door, and a seat on the right that could also serve as a child's bed. Beyond were small cupboards and shelves, more seating, the oil lamp, and at last a double bed across the width that folded up to allow a route through a door to the hold.

As mean as all this sounds, you had more space in a narrowboat cabin than you did in a caravan. Narrowboats were restricted in size by the locks they had to pass through, but the standard on most canals was 7ft wide, so a bargee family might only have had 10ft in length like the caravanners, but they had an extra 2ft or so in width.

The illustration shows a trading narrowboat, traditional except for its motive power, the diesel. Steam was tried but the reduction in load space, taken up by boilers and fuel, meant that the horse was not seriously challenged until a compact form of semi-diesel engine came in just before the First World War.

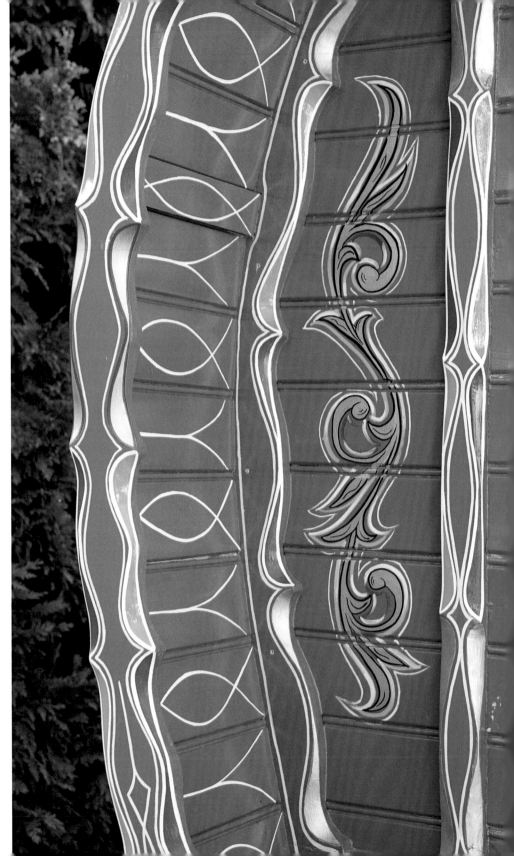

You can see travelling art at fairgrounds, so long as it has not been replaced by pictures of film stars and the like. Bright to the point of garish, geometrically abstract in background, often with illustrations of lions, tigers, motorcyclists, scantily clad females and so on; this is folk art with added showbiz.

After the fair, go to The Philharmonic pub in Liverpool, or The Princess Louise in High Holborn, London, or any pub from the mid- to late Victorian era that has managed to retain some of its original decor, and you will see variations on a theme they hold in common. Tiles, engraved glass, carved woodwork, the old murals if you are very lucky – all this is popular art, the art by which uneducated, unrefined, unpretentious people were uplifted and attracted.

The art of the gypsy caravan came from the same time, but was developed to an extent matched only by the pubs. While the brewers were spending huge amounts of money in order to bring in working people as customers, the gypsies were handing over relatively similar amounts, in terms of proportion of expenditure, on their status symbols.

The other difference, of course, was that gypsy art was highly personalised. What was popular had to be filtered through the gypsy taste, which meant that anything to do with horses was excellent, with added flash in the form of gold leaf, but the basis of the gypsy decorative tradition was what came naturally to the painters and carvers. What these Victorian craftsmen learned at their masters' benches, and

coincidentally what the gypsies liked, went back to Renaissance Italy and further.

The rebirth of the classical artistry of ancient Rome, for European woodcarvers at any rate, meant replacing the religious symbolism and narratives of the Gothic period with the designs the Romans had used when carving in marble. Compared with wood-carving that begins with and grows out of the nature of the material, to modern eyes such work, following the lines of stone bas-relief, may lack a certain spirited creativity. To the fifteenth-century craftsman, it was more than a breath of fresh air. It was a revolution, a new freedom from the grasp of the medieval.

Of course, wood has much more potential than marble for vitality, richness of detail, exuberant design and accurate naturalistic treatment, and the carvers began to take full advantage, achieving spectacular decorative effects with fantastic combinations of the real and the abstract. Instead of looking back and merely imitating the golden age of classicism, a newly lavish, sensuous, magnificent style emerged, as Italian notions spread and were developed to new levels of brilliance. Renaissance carving became Baroque.

The work that has lasted to modern times is, naturally enough, in churches and great houses. Go into St Paul's Cathedral in London and look at the work of Grinling Gibbons, on the Bishop's thrones and the Lord Mayor's seat. See his floral panels at Hampton Court. Gibbons was the master, possibly the greatest master we have had, but his trademark was, ultimately, his interpretation of the Roman sculptor's version of nature: of God's work, of the flowers, foliage, fruit, birds, fish and animals that, much later, were adapted by the Victorian carver to decorate the *vardo*.

The man working for Dunton's or Wright's kept to the same range of motifs as Gibbons: flowers, scrolls, acanthus leaves, egg and dart, bunches of grapes on the vine, birds. These figurative symbols acquired a reputation. They were supposed to have ancient gypsy magical significance, an idea that the gypsies did nothing to discourage, but they were no more mysterious than any off-the-shelf range of patterns. It was what the craftsman did with them that counted.

Every *vardo* was different but they had one thing in common. In every case, without exception, each and every *vardo*, if it was decorated at all, was 'lined out'.

Painted lines, typically in combinations of colours and thicknesses, followed the lines defined by the shapes of the different elements of the van. This was a technique and tradition long established in vehicle building in all its forms, from the finest ceremonial coach to the common street-trading cabriolet, from the brewer's dray to the two-wheeled handcart on the market square, and on to more modern forms of transport such as traction engines, but it surely found its greatest expression on the gypsy living waggon.

Look at a waggon's wheels, the small ones at the front, big ones at the back, crying out to have their elegance emphasised and accentuated. The rims, called the felloes, would take, let us say, a thin green outer line, then a thick yellow one bounded on both edges with red, then another green that dipped in at each spoke. Every spoke had four sides, so that was four opportunities for lining.

The steps up to the waggon from the road had to be tough for all the wear and tear they would get, but they had curved sides that never felt a foot, so here was another chance for lining, taking its inspiration from the curves in flowing waves and points. The shafts, long and thin, made a perfect medium, then you had the gutters, the weatherboards, the axle cases, all these functional basics of construction could be enhanced, not just by ordinary painting – unlike the bargemen, gypsies never did like a plain, flat, painted surface – but by painting and lining.

A gypsy chap of this writer's acquaintance presented three young cockerels as a gift. 'Surplus to requirements', he said to your correspondent. 'Roasting fowl.' They were put in a separate run, in case they were attacked by the resident chicken boss, a very large Rhode Island Red cock. A few days later, one of them lay dead. Thinking that perhaps a mink had penetrated security, their guardian placed the remaining two in with all the others. The horny spurs growing from the backs of their legs seemed exceptionally long but no conclusion was drawn from this interesting fact. A few more days later, a second one of them and the Rhode Island Red boss cock lay in wet heaps in corners of the run. The little fellow was indeed dead. The Rhodie was alive but much battered and dispirited, and missing an eye, while the last of the three roasting fowl strutted about, clearly in charge.

This story was related to their erstwhile owner in the pub. 'Ah,' he said. 'That'll be the one, then. I'll come round and pick him up tomorrow.'

Months later, apparently after several victories, the pub was entertained by a paradox. The bird had been raffled off in another pub, in the city, yet the owner still had him and was planning to fight him again. How could that be? 'Oh, I just put half the raffle money in my pocket, and bought him back off the winner with the other half.'

More than that, there were those parts of the waggon normally expected to become highly decorative features, such as the carved porch brackets, the door, the crown board (the curved board above the door), the pan box slung at the back – their decorations needed decorating. You might have had a pair of fighting cocks staring each other out on your yellow-painted pan-box doors, but they needed to be framed and put in context by red lining, plus a little gold and green scrollwork on the corners.

Lines, scrolls and curlicues were done freehand, preferably. Stencils and tracings might be employed sometimes but the result was never quite the same – so said the freehand exponents – never quite as lively and expressive as the work of the artistically wielded ox-hair or sable brush. Others might point out that, done freehand, opposing pairs of patterns never matched, and neither did repeated designs on either side of the waggon. So, you don't look at both sides at once – the freehanders said.

The thing about ox-hair brushes, used by modern sign writers and calligraphers as well as their Victorian ancestors, is that they are flexible, can carry the relatively thick paint (matt, not gloss), and keep their shape. The ones our artists used had their hairs gripped in a quill, just a short piece, which may explain why the sizes are named after birds. The smallest is a lark, then crow, duck, goose and swan. Today's signwriter can choose from rather more, up as far as a condor and including small duck and extra duck.

Without exception, every traditionally decorated *vardo* was 'lined out', that is, its shapes and structures were accented by painted lines, often in combinations of various widths and colours. Whether constructional basics such as wheel rims and spokes, shafts and gutters, or elaborate embellishments such as carved porch brackets, if it could take lining, it did.

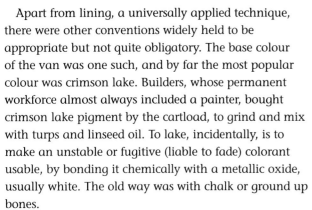

Apart from lining, a universally applied technique, there were other conventions widely held to be appropriate but not quite obligatory. The base colour of the van was one such, and by far the most popular colour was crimson lake. Builders, whose permanent workforce almost always included a painter, bought crimson lake pigment by the cartload, to grind and mix with turps and linseed oil. To lake, incidentally, is to make an unstable or fugitive (liable to fade) colorant usable, by bonding it chemically with a metallic oxide, usually white. The old way was with chalk or ground up bones.

The showmen initially liked to be different and preferred yellow as their predominant colour, but they mostly came around to crimson lake too. There was also an eccentric liking for green among some gypsies, on the grounds of camouflage, but this rather clashed with the overriding priority of status declaration by ornament.

Some standard decorative motifs were painted using a wooden template, cut with a fretsaw and used over and over. Horses running, horses standing, horses' heads, birds, flowers – these could be painted around, filled in and lined out, with time saved and

accuracy maintained for a repeated pattern. If the one commissioning the job could not afford so much carving, then these flat-painted designs would keep him suitably ornate.

A typical colour scheme for Reading, Ledge and Burton bodywork might be crimson lake for the tongue-and-groove boards or panels and the ribs, but with gold leaf and white lining on the ribs. The white was not brilliant white, of course, but the warm, white-not-quite called 'broken' white. Ribs were chamfered with long teardrop bevels, punctuated by short cuts called butterflies. Initially the idea had been to lighten the structure a little with a few longer chamfers, but the opportunity revealed for gold-leafing and lining produced a demand for more intricate and decorative work, as much as could be afforded.

Gold leaf was essential because the colour gold could not be done without, and there was no decent gold paint that would last. The leaf also would soon have been gone with the wind if left unvarnished, so that was done, although it meant dimming the glister of the gold slightly. Indeed, the whole waggon had a coat of varnish, or sometimes two, to protect the paintwork as well as the leaf.

There was no standard amount of gold leaf to be used. You would expect to see it on the rib chamfering and on the carvings between the ribs, on the crown boards and the porch brackets and, if there were lions' heads as gargoyles on the ends of the gutters, they might well have gold applied too. Stories are told about the wealthiest gypsies having 250 sq. ft of gold leaf applied to their caravans, a mind boggling amount and not just in price. While the commissioner of gilding would have had to shell out in 1920, at their prices, the equivalent of £4,000 in today's money for that amount of leaf, we have to bear in mind the labour involved.

Every little bit had to be glued on by hand, using French chalk all around to stop your leaf sticking anywhere it should not, and if it was on a carved surface it had to be brushed gently in to all the crevices. It is not an enormously difficult skill but it is slow, very slow. It was, and is, a most painstaking craft, and that £4,000 just for the material is probably an underestimate, since even the most careful and patient gilder would have expected to waste a third of his supply of leaf.

More likely, for a *vardo* gilded to a standard of flash and opulence sufficient to most requirements, the amount of leaf would have been more like 80 or 90 sq. ft, say 10 sq. yards, including wastage.

Underneath the body received almost as much attention, but without the gold leaf. Generally the colour of choice was a lemon or straw yellow, with just as much red, gold, green and white lining and

scrolling on, say, the axle casing as anywhere else on the waggon, despite the fact that it was bound to be covered in dirt from the road most of the time.

Painting and gold-leafing were hugely important as expressions of wealth and status, but carving was probably more so. There was carving on waggons from the 1850s onwards but the real heydays came after the turn of the century, when the intricacy and sheer amount of carving could become over ostentatious even for gypsy taste.

There were several basic essentials for carving, the chief of which being that it should not look stuck on. Apart from the pierced work, such as on porch brackets, all carving was indeed stuck on but it had to *look* as if it grew out of the wood of the van.

There also had to be a co-ordination about it, so that a waggon had a carving scheme, an over-all design with all elements fitting together. There might have been arguments about this, when the taste, or lack of it, in the buyer did not coincide with the experience and wisdom of the builder, and if the customer had his way then a certain vulgarity or over-flamboyance might spoil a beautifully made van.

The wood of choice for carving was generally sycamore. Other woods were used, by custom or request, such as wych elm, pitch pine, even mahogany, but everybody liked sycamore, always in plentiful supply and, with its qualities of fineness and strength, ideal for the job.

The other governing factor was, naturally, cost. Of course this varied over the years, but, if we assume that earnings kept pace with inflation, it is reasonably safe to pick a year as typical, let us say, 1920. A top of the range Reading, Ledge or Burton would have taken several months, maybe half a year, to build and would have cost the gypsy £150. This was the equivalent of £20,000 today. If you include the value of the horse, let us say £4,000 in modern money, that makes a favourable comparison with the £30,000 or £40,000 it would cost you now to buy a new, high-spec motorhome. The difference is that the motorhome has a very complex inside, with maybe three beds, luxury bathroom, fitted kitchen with sink and drainer, refrigerator, cocktail bar and flushing toilet, but a plain and rather ugly outside.

The gypsy ordering his horse-home in 1920 did not consider toilets and showers necessary, but he was very

interested in the price of carved porch brackets. On the Reading and the Ledge, particularly, it was standard to have elaborate double brackets on the front and single ones on the back. The cost of these altogether was around 10 per cent of the whole caravan. You are talking £2,000 modern, for something almost entirely non-functional. Well, let us say entirely non-functional, because so pierce-carved were they that they would keep no weather off the poor driver.

Add the lion-head gargoyles, the crown boards, the doors, all the carving on the bodywork between the ribs, and you could double that original £2,000 and we have not painted or gilded anything yet.

So important was the caravan as personal statement, that none but the poorest gypsies would have considered buying the basic waggon with no carving, no gold, no fancy painting, no luxuries inside, from a maker with no reputation, for £5,000 modern money. Furthermore, no gypsy, rich or poor, would have considered the money spent on porch brackets and gold leaf a waste. It was purely a matter of whether you could afford it.

While most builders had resident painters, they usually put the carving work out to specialists. Some carvers worked for more than one yard, adapting their work to that particular builder's style, although seldom straying from the standard patterns they knew so well. There might also be special instructions from the individual buyer, to be met as near as may be.

Once the raw waggon was built and the design scheme decided, the builder's craftsmen would cut

The colour picture shows a restored Open Lot waggon in traditional style and scheme. There is carving aplenty, but it looks the model of restraint compared to the Open Lot front shown in the monochrome picture. Clearly that has a fruity theme but someone seems to have forgotten the stricture of the carving not looking stuck on. We may or may not smile at the letter-plate, surely a joke, but overall we may think that the black and white lady is wearing too many jewels, whereas the colour lady has it just right.

the pieces of sycamore to the approximate sizes, offer them up on the waggon to check, and give each piece a number. The whole lot was delivered to the carver with detailed brief, and all the builder had to do when it came back was fix it by numbers to the van and call in his painters and gilders.

The wonderful world of porch brackets has three main varieties. The Burton waggons generally – but not always – had single brackets fore and aft, finely pierce-carved nonetheless. On the Ledge waggon, the bases for carved and painted brackets were often made by extending the matchboard bodywork to the front and back, cutting it to shape, and finishing the end of each board with a gold chamfer. A metal strengthener was fixed, then carved birds and so on applied on top. Certain makers such as William Wright were known for this technique, while others such as Dunton followed the same procedure as for a Reading van, which was to make the brackets separately.

The curve of the large front brackets lends itself to a circular motif and a lot of them had this, a ring with elaborate flower within, fitted as an opposing pair on either side of the van. More elegant designs came along in which the double front bracket became a single item, pierced, with sweeping curves and golden birds, blue grapes, red flowers and green leaves, the carved birds repeated elsewhere. We might say that here the art of the carvers, gilders and painters reached its zenith.

Looking at the front of the van, the eye is taken by two major features, the door and the curved lintel above it, called the crown board. Obviously the shape of the roof dictated the size of the crown board, so the Bowtops and Open Lots had smaller ones, Burtons had narrower ones, and the Readings and Ledges had the largest with the most scope for impressing. Usually there was a central motif, such as a horse's head, perhaps with associated horseshoe and whip, or a horse running, all with surrounding scrollwork, or an abstract pattern also with writhing scrolls and curls spreading from the centre.

Doors were the stable type, with carvings on the lower portion and the top in glazed halves. The lower part might be treated as one panel, with a central

pattern such as a lion's head surrounded by grapes and vine leaves, and a repeated design of flowers and scrollwork in the four corners. More usual was to have it in two or three panels, a narrow, horizontal one above with a flower and leaf carving perhaps, the larger square below with something floral or horsey or, if the square was in halves, a mirror image of birds – or something more exotic.

The most frequently seen door design these days seems to be the left-facing standing horse surrounded by trees and surmounted by central flower with acanthus leaves. This pattern possibly originated with the firm of Wright in the early 1900s. Certainly it can be seen in the old photographs taken at that time, and it is still here – see page 63, a restored Open Lot photographed at Appleby.

The most expensive waggons had carvings on and between every body rib, at the base, above and below a middle line, and at the top. Ledges had an extra line – base, above and below the jetty, above the middle line, and the top. Vans normally had nineteen ribs between the ends, the stanchions, giving twenty spaces for

Just the box for your pots and pans.

carvings, times four for the Reading, times five for the Ledge. Allowing for window and shutters, that leaves us eighty carvings on one side of a Ledge body, plus another twenty-eight on the front, thirty on the back, eighty on the other side, and that is without weatherboards, waistboards, chamfering on the ribs themselves, more carving on window boards, shutters, pan box, gargoyles, and not to forget horse's head butts (see page 93).

FOUR

STARTING WITH A VIVA

Rory Coxhill, self-taught *vardo* restorer, found he had a natural skill he had not known about when helping a friend customise a Vauxhall Viva with painted flames. That, and a life-long interest in fairground decor, carts and waggons, possibly inherited from costermonger ancestors, started him on the road to becoming one of the few full-time professional repairers and painters of all types of living waggon.

Another friend, one of his mother's who worked at the Ford Motor Co., gave him lessons in lining out, as an opportunity came up to buy a waggon. It was not a super-fancy Ledge with acres of gold leaf, but a simple Open Lot on artillery wheels. Even so, attempting restoration and repainting, Rory was very soon at the end of his knowledge, so he went to see a man who knows it all, John Pocket of Shropshire, to learn about scrolling, gilding and the other skills.

An Open Lot is a good place to start, and not just because it is a much simpler job than any of the straight-sided types. The roof of the Open Lot and the Bowtop gives them many advantages in longevity because they are less susceptible to two enemies, sun and rain, and not at all to a third, condensation. The curved roof keeps the rain off the unders, and, as there are no vertical ribs, there is nothing for the rain to run down into the cills to start the rot. There is much less painted woodwork to be exposed to the sun, which crazes varnish and cracks paint, letting the damp in underneath. And, because the Open Lot/Bowtop roof

Rory at work.

is lined inside the waggon with carpet or other thick fabric, there is no condensation, a serious plague of the straight-sided ones.

We have to say also that the Open Lot is by far the most likely type of *vardo* to be available for restoration, partly because it is the most recent design and so has had fewer years to last, but also because it has proved to be the most practical. While the straight-sided models looked the most brilliant in all their finery, the plainer, sturdier Open Lot and Bowtop, with their lower centres of gravity, were much less likely to tip over. Generally, too, they were much lighter, and so less liable to get stuck in the mud or sink halfway to their hubs overnight on the village green, with attendant

panicking horse as she breaks the splinter bar in her efforts to pull the waggon out and suddenly finds herself free and galloping down the high street.

Other reasons for shortages of the older types include less than perfect workmanship and skimping on materials. For example, elsewhere in this book we have stated that unders were made of ash. This was certainly the case in theory, and in the best practice, but, in even the most famous yards, it was not unknown to confine the use of ash to those parts of the unders directly connected to metalwork, and to make the rest of pine.

No matter how well made a waggon might have been, it could not withstand a fire. A waggon went up like a torch, and fires were often deliberate, it being

the custom to burn the waggons of senior figures in the gypsy community who had died. This was not a cremation; the deceased would be buried according to custom. It was more to do with destroying the possessions of the dead so that the spirit could be free from earthly bonds. A symbolic heap of possessions might still be burned today by traditional families, but probably not a rare *vardo*.

For working on, too, the bowed types are better. You can take the roof right off and make it easy to repair and fix the furniture and fittings. Compare that with the complexities of the 1925 Burton that Rory is restoring for a gypsy family. That a waggon of such an age is here at all is largely because the roof rails were specified in mahogany when it was built, probably in Kent and possibly in a boatyard with a humorous workforce. Taking off some wooden panels for repair, Rory found them painted with the words 'port' and 'starboard'.

Often, and for obvious reasons as with any house, the roof is where trouble starts, and, if not fixed in time, is the cause of complete downfall. If the roof of an old waggon has deteriorated, you can look at the cills (also called summers or carriers) and expect to find them soft and rotten. Such a waggon has no chassis for its bodywork. Rather than try and repair it, you may as well build a new one.

The mahogany and other hardwoods, a luxurious inside and an extra strong and bulky unders, makes this particular Burton an impossible pull for one horse. It was meant to be taken from fairground to fairground by traction engine or petrol lorry. Two shire horses would struggle to get it up a hill with family and possessions aboard and, doubtless, a useful and naturally heavy stove.

The twenty books of gold leaf Rory will use will not weigh much. Each book has 320 sq. in of leaf in twenty

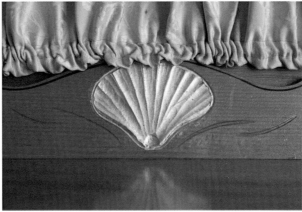

leaves; twenty books is just short of 45 sq. ft, about half
the average used in the good old days, but in the good
old days gold did not cost over $1,000 an ounce. Nor
will the 'carving' weigh heavy because these days it
is stick-on fibreglass. A one-man firm in the north of
England has spotted this market and produces standard
patterns such as birds and bunches of grapes, copied
from the old designs. It is up to people like Rory how
they make them look like the real thing and part
of their background, which can be done with pains,
lining and lots of coats of paint. You can also find
self-adhesive horses on the internet because, for some
unfathomable reason, American truck drivers like to
decorate their rear windows with them.

  Ah yes, the paint. Well, for a start, you cannot buy
truly suitable paint or varnish in any DIY store or ships'
chandlers. No modern paint is in the right colours,
and, even if it is almost in the proper red, green,

yellow and white, it will be gloss, so unsuitable, and lead-free, and so without the ability to last through our winters and summers. Nor does any mainstream paint manufacturer produce the correct shade of crimson lake.

Yacht varnish will not do either. Caravan varnish has to be a special 98 per cent reflective, modified alkyd product, which is a development of one of those polyputakettlon chemicals but made from plants rather than petroleum, and it is flexible when dry, so, when the sun shines and the wood shrinks, it is less liable to crack.

For paint, it has to be lead based and it has to be in many coats as well as many colours. When flat-painting a panel on an Open Lot, Rory Coxhill will first put down two coats of lead-based white undercoat then, because his speciality is oak lookalike scumbling, he will be using yet more specialist coatings.

The fundamentals of the art of scumbling are to lay down a base colour in the same range as the natural colour of the wood being imitated, then to put over it a darker glaze which is manipulated when wet, allowing the base colour partly to show through, to create the graining effect. Thus, for oak the base colour is an off-white, the glaze a specific light oak colour or dark oak. Mahogany effect is achieved with a reddish base and a mahogany glaze, and these tend to be the only two woods imitated on waggons.

The first tool used on the wet glaze is the flogging brush, a big heavy object like a very coarse whitewash brush. More delicate tools are the overgraining brush, the heartwood graining tool called a rocker, and various combs. One coat of varnish finishes that part of the job.

Some parts of the board will be covered in a colour, say bright green, and some areas will be left to show the oak graining. On the green bits, Rory will apply three coats of green undercoat and two of top green. Scrolling, or whatever decoration is planned, is drawn on first with chalk and tracing paper, and then painted and gilded. Finally, on go three coats of varnish over the whole board.

Every painter has a style. Some say Rory's is too 'fairground', which he vigorously denies and partially admits at the same time. On the Bowtop with the

cherries, greyhounds will be painted where horses
might be expected, with a leaping hare, in tune with
the traditional travellers' interest in hare coursing. The
cherries, incidentally, can be traced back to the first
of the traveller painters, Jimmy Berry, who copied a
design from a 'Cherry Blossom' brand boot-polish tin
lid and used it as his signature, since he could not read
or write.

So, you have painted your waggon and want to get on
the road. You have a problem. The horse, by which your
waggon was meant to be pulled, does not exist. Before
the First World War there were millions of carriage
horses everywhere, but the end was in sight. The last of

London's horse-drawn omnibuses ran in 1911. Not long
after the end of that war, in which so many horses were
killed, the internal combustion engine had replaced the
horse in pretty well all forms of transport throughout
the developed world. The carriage horse, larger than
a cob or pony, smaller than a shire, had gone from
indispensible omnipresence to not being needed at all.

The gypsies stopped using it in the 1960s when the
fashion came in for the black and white fell-pony
types, known as 'coloured horses'. There are plenty of
these about and they can pull a waggon all right. Oh,
and that paint. It costs about ten times as much as
normal paint.

FIVE

FAIR ENOUGH?

Without the gypsy-led continuance of the horse fairs, the gypsy *vardo* would have disappeared from public view long ago, except for a few museum specimens, but the fairs are dying. Just as the gypsies have kept the fairs going, so the fairs have allowed some sort of prolonging of the travelling life and the upkeep of its most spectacular achievement, the living waggon as art. The question is, where and when will it all end, for end it surely must.

Of late, many traditionally minded travelling folk have switched from troublesome fairs to the peace and tranquillity of the steam engine rallies, there to meet and gossip and admire, and to be alongside gatherings of caravan enthusiasts, painters and restorers, people not necessarily with travelling backgrounds and not necessarily keen on horses but all keen on the glory of the *vardo*. This gives renewed hope for the long life of caravan art, as we watch the fairs sink.

We have mentioned the fairs at Appleby-in-Westmorland and Stow-on-the-Wold as opportunities to see gypsy waggons. There are other fairs too, for example at Priddy in Somerset, but the general trend is downwards in various ways.

A small exception seems to be the fair at Seamer, near Scarborough, entirely defunct not many years ago but now seeing something of a revival. At the time of writing, the authorities are arranging for an open-field site in expectation of up to a hundred caravans and accompanying vehicles, horses and whatnot. The previous year, the designated site was judged inappropriate by the fair attenders and the result was chaos, featuring forty-four caravans almost everywhere except where they were supposed to be. The council, trying to please everybody in the face of several hundred objections from people living in the village, are hoping they have done enough to keep control, to assure a smooth passage for the event which almost everybody, apart from the travelling guests, would rather did not happen at all.

Seamer Fair, like every fair, began with a royal charter granting the local bigwig or bigwigs the

The road to Appleby.

right to hold what amounted to a grand market, with attendance fees payable to said bigwig. These early charters were only granted where safe passage and conduct of the fair could be guaranteed by the grantees, so that presupposed a powerful local lord such as a baron, or bishop perhaps.

The root of the word fair is in the Latin word *feriae*, meaning days of rest, holidays or festivals. Although the word in English really means – as the *Oxford English Dictionary* puts it – 'a periodical gathering of buyers and sellers, in a place and at a time ordained by charter or statute or by ancient custom', there has always been an element of festivity and amusement about it which, originally, was secondary to the main purpose of trade. The idea of fairs came over with the Conqueror; there had been great fairs in France, for instance in Champagne and Brie, for hundreds of years.

Now the groups of ponies are in clusters, all with their heads to the centre. When a spectator signifies his desire to see one in particular the owner gives a rough order to his drover, who dashes at the indicated animal, pulls it out by the tail, and runs it down a narrow alley in the crowd, grasping its mane. Sometimes the terrified animal does not stop at the end of the human avenue, and there is hurry-scurry, and now and again a fall in the mud and much merriment. Sometimes a very obstinate brute will take half a dozen men to detach him from his comrades, and then make much demur to running the gauntlet of switches and whips. These colts are the chief centres of attraction, for not only is most business done in them, but the many idlers get much amusement out of the hurly-burly.

The Dalesman, A. Wren Rumney, 1911.

This is an eye-witness account of Brough Hill Fair, held last day of September and first of October, where scores of gypsy horse-dealers congregated to supply the local market of farmers and gentlefolk, watched by crowds of idlers from the industrial cities of Yorkshire and Lancashire, along for a day out. In earlier times there would have been great numbers of sheep and cattle too, especially Highland cattle, but by 1910 or so it was mostly down to its long-time specialisation in unbroken fell ponies.

Our photograph shows the calmer atmosphere prevailing on a quiet horse-trading day at Appleby New Fair, where the dealers sell only to each other. It is only a few miles from Brough but still going, when all that is left of its neighbour is an expression, still used: 'Brough Hill weather', which is 'clashy' in the local dialect, or cold, wet, windy and miserable to the rest of us.

Whereas King Richard II on the eleventh day of November in the sixth year of his reign in the year of our Lord one thousand three hundred and eighty two did grant unto the Lords of the Manor and to their heirs for ever one fair yearly to be kept in the said Manor upon the fifteenth day of July being Saint Martin his day and so to continue for the space of seven days. By virtue of which grant and confirmation thereof from time to time we do openly proclaim and publish and declare that this fair beginning on the fifteenth day of July and so for seven days following except the Lord's Day it shall and may be lawful for all and every person and persons resorting to this fair to buy sell and bargain or deal in any lawful goods wares merchandise horses geldings mares colts fillies beasts sheep or any other cattle whatsoever paying unto the Lords of the Manor by his officers appointed to receive the same pollage package stallage standage and other duties belonging to him for the same. And we do in the King his Majesty's name straitly charge and command all manner of persons whatsoever coming and resorting to this fair that they keep the peace during this fair and in the end so to depart. God save the King and the Lord of the Manor.

Pollage was a levy on numbers, an entry fee per head. Package was a tax on amounts of commodities sold, like a kind of purchase tax, so the seller would know that for every sack of wool he sold, or every two pigs or twenty hens, he would have to pay the fair owner a fee. If that was, say, three pennies, about £5 in today's money, the seller would obviously have that in mind when agreeing his sale price.

Stallage was exactly what you might expect, a levy on stall-holders, and standage was another name for the same thing. All this was part of the tax regime of the time. Nobody had really thought through the possibilities of taxing income or wealth directly. Such a system would have been too difficult to manage anyway, but the ruling classes had to be supported somehow. It was the feudal duty of the lower orders to keep the rich rich. Wealth was land, and the lords of manors had the produce of that land and the rents from those who farmed the land at their lords' pleasure, but a little extra cash never went amiss. Lords were always happy to have fairs and markets where money changed hands right there, under their noses, so a proportion could be skimmed off without too much trouble.

We note that the purpose of the fair is the buying and selling of lawful goods and animals. It is a market. All fairs are markets, but not all markets are fairs – so this is a seven-day, once-a-year market on a kind of scale to attract traders and customers from far and wide. Goods not available at the ordinary markets would be here, at the fair, perhaps including wares and merchandise brought by some of the increasing number of traders from overseas.

Two important features of fairs in later years are missing. There is no mention of the labour-hiring function, where farmers took on men and women to work for a set time on agreed terms, because in 1382 we were still in the feudal era and there were not so many free men and free women to hire. Also, there is no mention of the entertainment side of things, but there never was in these charters. Fairs themselves attracted all manner of persons whatsoever, without any need for a formal invitation, but these did not include gypsies at first because, in England anyway, there were none.

Even so, when gypsies did start arriving, these fairs were irresistible to them. Just as the lord of the manor saw his fair as a payday, so did the gypsies. Of course, they were very interested in trading mares, colts, fillies and so on, but they were also entertainers and fortune-tellers. Over the years, fairs and gypsies formed a kind of love match. You could not have one without the other, and, gradually, the fairs acquired another special function. They became the tribal meeting places

for travelling folk who did not see much of each other
normally. Marriages were arranged, gossip was traded,
old acquaintance renewed. Eventually, after centuries of
this, it could only be a small step for the gypsies to begin
to think that fairs had been arranged entirely for their
convenience, that their assemblies at fairs were more
than a tradition. They had become a right. The charter
set up the fair, the gypsies kept it going, QED.

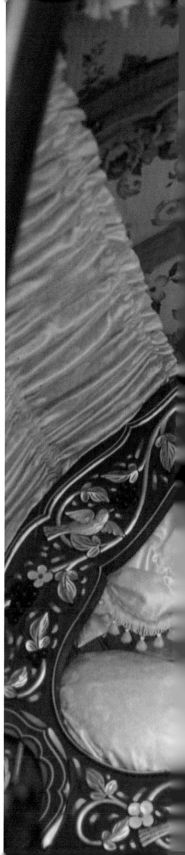

RIOTOUS SCENES AT SEAMER. VILLAGERS AND POTTERS DO BATTLE.

Not for many years has Seamer Fair been marred by such scenes of rowdyism and misconduct as characterised it on Saturday. There was an unparalleled outbreak at night, but also during the day as a whole there occurred serious injuries to several villagers.

The original cause appears to have been as follows. Two Seamer men entered the Londesborough Arms. Several potters or gypsies, visiting the fair, whose caravans were in a field at the village, were having a sing song. The two Seamer men were talking together and the potters called for order. The villagers did not comply and in the ensuing general scuffle the potters were ejected and allowed themselves to be conducted to their caravans.

Later, a body of 40 or 50 villagers proceeded towards the potters' camp at Manor Field. The potters hurled hot cinders and bricks, and 12 of their womenfolk, armed with iron bars, made an ugly rush at the villagers.

The villagers did not stand to meet the attack and the arrival of the police prevented more serious consequences.

The charter quoted on page 83 is the one for Seamer Fair. By 1937, the *Scarborough Evening News* was reporting a fair 'smaller than the fairs of long ago' but still attracting visitors and holidaymakers, and 'prominent among the crowd were large numbers of gypsies'.

The Second World War interrupted the fair to such an extent that by 1952, 'The horse fair proper has not been held for some years, but this evening horse racing will take place in a field'. Two years later there were no gypsies on fair day, and by 1961 the only trading in goods, wares and merchandise was a WI stall. It is not recorded whether the good ladies of the WI paid the Lord of the Manor his due stallage and package. The Lordship was by then bought and sold anyway. For a price, the title brought a few small pieces of grass verge on the village street and the customary privilege of distributing largess to the poor, in this case five quid's worth of copper coins thrown for the school children, who had the morning off.

One horse dealer turned up on the off chance in 1962 in 'his gaily painted caravan', and that was that until recently. Now, a hundred caravans might arrive, gaily painted or not, and those villagers looking forward with mixed feelings to the 2011 fair might be interested to read the report of the fair exactly a century before. This (left) is the *Scarborough Evening News* in July, 1911.

At least two things are clear from this report. First, it almost goes without saying that the gypsies were in caravans. Second, although order usually ruled at the fair, strong feelings were simmering beneath and it did not take much for them to boil over.

Residents of Appleby and Stow will recognise this very well. Certainly Appleby in recent years has seen rowdiness and misconduct aplenty, to such an extent that many of the long-standing fair-goers, the ones who consider themselves genuine gypsies, are not attending, in their gaily painted caravans or at all. Appleby in 2009 saw armed police for the first time, and a massive operation against drug dealers who had come in from the big cities.

What seems to have happened is that the crowds and the slightly organised chaos of the typical fair have attracted a new class of visitor. This is the modern version, the ugly and menacing replacement for the horse dealer, the juggler, the trinket seller, the fortune-teller and the pick-pocket. This visitor does not care to be straightly charged and commanded to keep the peace. He takes the short-term view and sees an opportunity to bargain or deal in unlawful goods, wares and merchandise. The trouble is, he will kill the goose that lays the golden eggs. He will destroy the fair.

In pre-Victorian times, there were several thousand fairs. Most have already disappeared through natural causes, replaced by shops in the high street, goods transported everywhere at all times by road, rail and air, auction marts and seven-days-a-week all-night supermarkets. We do not need to go anywhere once a year to buy anything, so there is no point in the sellers assembling either, and only a very few of us want a horse. And if the *gadjo* did want a horse, would he feel comfortable buying one at a fair?

However, the fairs at Appleby, Stow and elsewhere still attract many thousands of 'visitors and holidaymakers'. They might purchase souvenirs at the market stalls but that is not why they come. They come to look at the funny gypsies, their horses and their caravans, and the gypsies are happy to oblige with a show, because, without the tourist mobs, the fairs would die all the quicker. The gypsies cannot pretend any longer that their purpose at the fair is to

do business, with each other and the general populace, therefore, the fair itself has no purpose other than the show. It is a fun-fair, but instead of taking rides on the waltzer we can watch horses being washed in the river.

The fairs that are left can easily be abolished. Contrary to accepted gypsy opinion, they as a group have no rights at all connected with fairs. Leaving aside the fun-fairs – such as the Nottingham Goose Fair – that have replaced the traditional annual market, it has been the case that the few surviving fairs owe their continued existence to the gypsies, but that is all. Charters were granted to lords of manors or the burghers of a town, not to the 'all manner of persons whatsoever' who might come there.

Also contrary to widely held opinion, it does not require an Act of Parliament to extinguish a fair. The Home Secretary can do it, with the permission of the owner of the fair, that is, the successor of the charter grantee. See Appendix, The Fairs Act 1871.

The Act begins with these words: 'Whereas certain of the fairs held in England and Wales are unnecessary, are the cause of grievous immorality, and are very injurious to the inhabitants of the towns in which such fairs are held'.

Armed police? Drug dealers? Injurious indeed, and what possible place can gaily painted caravans have among that lot?

APPENDIX

THE FAIRS ACT, 1871

Whereas certain of the fairs held in England and Wales are unnecessary, are the cause of grievous immorality, and are very injurious to the inhabitants of the towns in which such fairs are held, and it is therefore expedient to make provision to facilitate the abolition of such fairs:

1

TITLE

This Act may be cited as 'The Fairs Act 1871'.

2

DEFINITION OF 'OWNER'

In this Act the term 'owner' means any person or persons, or body of commissioners, or body corporate, entitled to hold any fair, whether in respect of the ownership of any lands or tenements, or under any charter, letters patent, or Act of Parliament, or otherwise howsoever.

3

SECRETARY OF STATE

Who may, on representation of magistrates, with consent of owner, order fair to be abolished. Notice of representation to be published in newspapers.

In case it shall appear to the Secretary of State for the Home Department, upon representation duly made to him by the magistrates of any petty sessional district within which any fair is held, or by the owner of any fair in England or Wales, that it would be for the convenience and advantage of the public that any such fair shall be abolished, it shall be lawful for the said Secretary of State for the Home Department, with the previous consent in writing of the owner for the time being of such fair, or of the tolls or dues payable in respect thereof, to order that such fair shall be abolished accordingly: Provided always, that notice of such representation, and of the time when it shall please the Secretary of State for the Home Department to take the same into consideration, shall be published once in the *London Gazette*, and in three successive weeks in some one and the same newspaper published in the county, city, or borough in which such fair is held, or if there be no newspaper published therein, then in the newspaper of some county adjoining or near thereto, before such representation is so considered.

4

ORDER OF SECRETARY OF STATE TO BE PUBLISHED IN NEWSPAPER

When and so soon as any such order as aforesaid shall have been made by the Secretary of State for the Home Department, notice of the making of the same shall be published in the *London Gazette*, and in some one newspaper of the county, city, or borough in which such fair is usually held, or if there be no newspaper published therein, then in the newspaper of some county adjoining or near thereto, and thereupon such fair shall be abolished.